BOOK SOLD

On Not Losing
My Father's Ashes
in the Flood

On Not Losing

My Father's Ashes

in the Flood

Richard Harrison

A Buckrider Book

Buckrider Books is an imprint of Wolsak and Wynn Publishers.

Cover and interior design: Natalie Olsen, Kisscut Design
Cover image © Aubord Dulac / Shutterstock.com
Author photograph: Keeghan Rouleau
Typeset in Seria Text and Ideal Sans
Printed by Coach House Printing Company Toronto, Canada

 Canada Council **Conseil des Arts**
for the Arts du Canada

 Canadian Patrimoine
Heritage canadien

 ONTARIO ARTS COUNCIL
CONSEIL DES ARTS DE L'ONTARIO
an Ontario government agency
un organisme du gouvernement de l'Ontario

The publisher gratefully acknowledges the support of the Canada Council for the Arts, the Ontario Arts Council and the Canada Book Fund.

Buckrider Books
280 James Street North
Hamilton, ON
Canada L8R 2L3

Library and Archives Canada Cataloguing in Publication
Harrison, Richard, 1957–, author
On not losing my father's ashes in the flood / Richard Harrison.
Poems.
ISBN 978-1-928088-22-6 (paperback)
I. Title.
PS8565.A6573O56 2016   C811'.54   C2016-904666-4

For
Lisa

Contents

On Not Losing My Father's Ashes in the Flood / 1

A Poem in the Arms of Tyrannosaurus Rex / 3

Gone / 5

This Son of York / 7

The World Made New / 9

Slinky / 11

Now is the Winter / 13

Descartes, or "Lightcrawler" / 14

Poem for a Crescent Moon / 16

Found Poem / 18

When: A Love Poem / 20

Jack Kirby / 22

Superman / 23

Apostrophe / 25

Archive / 27

Small as God / 29

Just So Story / 31

Propaganda / 33

Just Who Do You Fuckers Think You Are? / 34

Colour Code / 36

Ghost Wood / 38

Cell Phone / 40

Spoken Word / 42

Confessional Poem / 44

Greatness / 46

With the Dying of the Light / 47

Ode to a Temporary Urn / 49

The Creative Writing Teacher Writes to His Wife / 50

Borges: "The Riddle of Poetry" / 51

A Home on Al-Mutanabbi Street / 52

More Sex, More Nature / 53

The Golden Age / 54

Epic / 56

Saddledome: After the Flood / 57

Under Western Water: Returning to Work / 60

Maps and Writing Paper / 63

Skype / 64

This Poem is Alive Because it is Unfinished / 65

A Poem is a Story that Sometimes Happens to Someone / 67

Birthday Card / 69

Prayer / 70

The Wonder of Life / 71

Mulligan / 72

Haiku / 73

ACKNOWLEDGEMENTS 79   NOTES 81

On Not Losing My Father's Ashes in the Flood

We couldn't find my father's ashes
during the flood of 2013
and thought they had been swept away. Or maybe

one of the volunteers, there only to do good, saw the jar
that held them covered with silt and threw it out,
as it went with so many things people cared for
in the buried treasure of their homes –

                              family photographs,
                                   manual typewriters, diplomas under glass.

After the river left our house, two of my wife's friends
took apart our piano, which was waterlogged
                              and could not be saved.

And the piano, being demolished, made a concert
from the jugular grief of crowed wood, the broken memory of glue
and the squeal of screws no longer holding fast.

It ended with the crash of the great harp
onto a crib of concrete,   a zoo in panic,
every note the piano knew climaxed at once,

                          every animal howling
                      as the river rose in their cages.

At the news of my father's ashes lost to the water,
my neighbours winced like something wild
had eaten a pet they'd all fed from their hands.

But a friend from Poland thought it was hilarious,
and so did I – we both come from a long line of cannon fodder.

Dad would've laughed, too. I'd kept his ashes
because nothing I'd thought to do with them was right. He used to say,
If you wait, things will solve themselves –
the trick is knowing when to wait.

I was reading Robert Hass's elegy
for his younger brother – with Robert's mind caught up
                    imagining a funeral
in which his brother's body was burned on a boat in the river,

so first the fire, and then the air, and then, finally,
the river took the body – as if downstream
                    was another word for heaven.

We found the jar
in a box of books and a remote-controlled car
taken to the kitchen
when everyone grabbed everything above the waterline;
                    it had never been touched by the river.

And now it sits on a shelf in my living room,
my father's ashes not taken by the flood
that I will not give to the air
until I have learned all he has to teach me
                    with the last part of the earth that was him.

A Poem in the Arms of Tyrannosaurus Rex

I was a boy when the dinosaurs
dragged their dead-weight tails
through the museums of knowledge:
> so suffocating their mass, the marvel of it was they lived at all.

But by the time I got to university, they had evolved:
those tails rose from the mud and stuck straight out like yardarms,
and they did a yardarm's work;
> the old monsters leapt up and raced, sleek Olympians.

Out with the Frankensteinian shuffle and moan,
in with hotfooting it after a jeep and roaring like three tenors into an oil drum.

And now that I am the age of my students' fathers,
the terrible lizards have clothed themselves in brilliant feathers –
> them and all their descendants who hatch from the symbols of birth
> and grow, singing, into the symbols of freedom.

Everything changes, even extinction.

But through it all, a constant – the tiny arms of Tyrannosaurus Rex.
Everybody loves those arms,
part puzzle, part mystery, part joke –
> hands that reach neither mouth nor prey,
> ridiculous limbs that interrupt the symmetry
of an otherwise streamlined aesthetic,
> like the penis of a naked man in profile.

Someday, check out the skeleton of a whale.
There are leg bones there, tucked in the flesh
like bits of shrapnel no one bothered to remove,
                a fact you know but never use in conversation.

What if those Tyrannosaurus arms never showed,
        but stayed, creased upon themselves,
remembering the time when the rest of the body wasn't
so pure and efficient that it could strike with a neck like a bullwhip,
crush and pound with trip-hammer legs,
        and lay open a Triceratops with its jackknife jaws alone?

What if, inside that chest,
        the Tyrant King folded his secret hands in vestigial prayer?

What would we have to laugh at then?
How else could we make the terrifying monarch of life
        into a caricature of us,
        who have lived so briefly
                        where he reigned so long?

Gone

When the groom's mother died on the way to the wedding in San Diego,
　　　　　it became a wedding from an American novel.

Everyone took the lead
and no one agreed on how it should end
　　　　　so we focused on the purpose of each day –

　　　　　　　　　　What else could we do?

Sometimes that purpose was the wedding on the beach,
sometimes it was the mother's body still in Utah where she died.

Everything fell into place as if it had been written –
　　　　　　　which does not mean everything went well; it means
　　　　　　　it seemed like an imagination was at work
　　　　　　　the way the absurd makes you think life is fiction.

It was an American novel right down to the road trip because
American literature is about grief spread over space.

Instead of the honeymoon,
the bride and groom drove his mother's ashes back from the desert,
taking the long way and photographs with the ashes
　　　　in front of the Grand Canyon and the Mandalay Bay Resort and Casino,
　　　which she had planned to see on the ride home.

We all carry the story, and we tell it to anyone who asks,
How was your summer? expecting the usual,
Good.

But it was not good, and you can only tell so many lies,
so everyone who was there found their own way to talk about it –
sometimes with the surprise up front,
sometimes in the middle
or setting the whole thing up for laughs
                    with the dark twist at the end –
          because characters in a novel can escape anything
                              except their story.

I've surrounded myself with information, facts,
          and every day the same pop song about
                    absence lingering in the fragmented heart
                         plays itself over and over in my brain.

And I barely knew her.

People are making lists – Update your will. What will you leave your children?

My wife's sister, tired of her quarrels, packed up her family
                              and moved right across the compass.

But the way I see it, a song stuck in your head is
your mind reaching for poetry like a drowning mouth reaching for air,
and you never know how beautiful air, or light, or life are until you must gasp.

This Son of York

All the world's a phrase,
and of all the phrases in the world, my father loved best
            Now is the winter of our discontent
            made glorious summer by this son of York.

It sprung from his lips I know not how oft,
and it leapt among the last he said
the day they mended his shattered hip, and,
fearing his heart would fail on the table,
the doctors asked me what they should do.

My father's will was the last whole thing he had, I knew:
            Let him go, I said, and signed the page.

And then I walked to where he waited and took his hand.

Now is the winter of our discontent,
        he began again, his voice with Shakespeare
made glorious summer.

It has taken me all this time to ask, why
those words and not some others – or his own?

And I have written of him having a divine and terrible beauty
                                I could not help but praise.

My father answered with this soliloquy that
begins the play where Richard, who would be Third,
though not yet king, humpbacked, gross and loathing
every beautiful thing he beautifully describes,
longs for war's reprise when he,
rudely stamped, unfit for love or joy,
could be monarch among men at their monstrous height.

My father longed, too,
for the days of youth and war
as the last time in his life he knew exactly what to do.

What comes to me now is how out of place a man
such longings make,
> how little peace could offer him when he put down the gun,
>> and all the words he lived by then lay down their meaning beside it.

And all my writing around his name became a losing argument for the beauty
of a man who found beauty everywhere but in himself.

My father taught me a poem is not its words, but the ringing it leaves behind.

And when my father from his hospital bed spoke the usurper's lines who
put every molecule of rage into laying waste to what he saw,
I understood it then: my father was never reciting this precipitous rant,
> he was rewriting it,
replacing every word with one that reads the same but means the opposite.

He looked me full in the face, the way I look at my own daughter and my son,
glorious summer he's said to me for almost half a century,
and with that clutch of words
> this son of York held on.

The World Made New

When he realized that he would never leave the Home,
        my father was as furious as
    a man with a memory refined to minutes could be.

He flared out in short blasts at the knowledge,
then faded just as fast into puzzlement at where he was.

Then he'd figure it out again.

Watching him was like watching fireflies in a forest,
      each one a fragment of light,
but not so great a light to keep away the darkness
                      that gives the light its meaning.

My father felt betrayed by the doctors who'd
repaired his busted hip, and for him, the old soldier,
        betrayal was the greatest of sins.

It would only be a matter of time
before he'd forget the origin of his presence
among them who slept in their chairs to the soundtrack of the TV,

and though he never believed that he had always been there,
eventually he understood that dying was his only escape
from the piece of shit body he declared he had left.
The worst part was the argument
to explain the memory he no longer had
because you need a memory to grasp your memory's loss.

I asked him about the day when he, filled with gratitude
for the surgeons, looked for something of himself to give to the intern
who was with him when he woke,

        and, owning nothing else,
   he took the ruined ball joint of his leg that
        they had cut away so he could walk,
and offered that.

He answered he remembered, but when I asked
what he remembered later, he did not know,
and denied I posed a question.

Around we'd go
   in that darkness together –
      trapped in that terrible excellence
       poets long for in every poem

   that moment words have no past and in them is the world made new.

Slinky

I thought I was a patient man,
        but then I watched my son play with a Slinky
                when he was eight years old.

He played with the toy for an hour,
        the way children do when we're not looking.

When the rare adult captures such play,
say on stage, improvising with a sock turned into
        a missing dog that's made its way home,
                and we feel that reunion though nothing was lost,
        we say it is art, maybe even genius.

But it is memory refusing to let go.

My son's turned the Slinky into a yo-yo,
he's made it step from the bed to the door
and coaxed it until it could do what the commercials never show –
                take one more step along the horizon of the floor.

Then he shows me his favourite game:
curling the metal rings into a small arch, like the back of an armadillo,
and just petting it, the Slinky moving under his fingertips like
the back of an animal comforted by human touch.

The Slinky was invented at sea, in war.
A mechanical engineer saw a spring fall from its place
        on his shelf, then shimmy with the roll of the ocean
     down the staircase of books
          beside his desk.

He felt again the pleasure of the child he once was,

took it home,

and told his wife, *I can make it walk.*

But then my son holds the metal spiral aslant so

the coils line up like a row of dimes

removed from a roll and lying on the table.

He tells me he can see himself

in the mirror their shiny sides become.

Then he shows me my own face in this plaything I grew up with

but was never patient enough to see.

Now is the Winter

With the last ounces of his grace, my father
stands up from his wheelchair, turns toward
the bed as though the floor is ice;
he tilts his spine, knees bent, and waits to shift
his weight to mine; I lay him on the blanket
and kiss his lips. We talk of Shakespeare
who carried him line by line through tropic wars
to the final surgery on his failing hips.
Now is the winter of our discontent,
he recites from those pages of his brain
no disease has yet erased,
the words the prayer of one
who has no god to hear his cries, his powers spent.
When he asks, I promise to be with him when he dies,
and winter stirs in the broken fingers
of my hand that long ago healed winter cold
into mended bone. My father sleeps as the land sleeps –
and I am taught that nothing is immortal
and awake forever. Outside, the heroes, green,
and knowing only what they see,
take their sticks and pucks and
lean into their shots
while the mid-winter's night
dreams water turned to stone beneath their feet.

Descartes, or "Lightcrawler"

When no one is measuring time,
    and my young son greets the morning curled up under his green comforter
like a monarch in its chrysalis, his mind
    is fluid and slow and changing
        into something other than it was in his dreams.

At times like this, I can lie beside him in the big bed where
he is learning sleep, and read in the page of sunlight
    he allows to be slipped into his room sideways through the window.

It's a slow time – time for dust in the air like gulls above parkland,
           particles of dust catching the light – or caught by it – then gone.

It's the time of day he wrote his first poem,
pushing his mother away from the door, saying,
    Don't come in, and writing

    Lightcrawler

    I woke up facing the curtain
    and saw the light crawling out
    from the curtain then pounce
    and kill the darkness.

He showed us the poem –
    in crayon on a notepad – and warned us,
Don't expect any more.

We didn't protest.
Morning is no time for such promises.

My back slips into the gravity at the surface of his mattress
    the way a stack of cards
        brushed aside
            makes a little ramp on the table,
                a curve composed of straight lines, and that's its beauty.

I am reminded that the famous Descartes
discovered the axis between X and Y
while watching the sunlight mark its progress in
horizons of light it drew where his walls met.

I can see him lying in bed
while the numbers fell from the air,
        and the monks outside his door waited for
            the notoriously late sleeper
                        to stop shining – and rise.

Now I have a reason for this knowledge,
and a home for it. Almost everything we have
comes from dreams brought over the edge of
an open eye into the waking day.

My son rolls under the duvet,
    and I talk to him in the voices of his stuffed toys.
They know their planet: a giant lives beneath the ground.

Poem for a Crescent Moon

You can feel them,
        moving,
                words like elephants over the dusty earth,
words for the glass of water on my desk,
    words for death
        and mourning
           and philosophy, and the question
           of my fingertips spread over your thigh while you're driving.

I want them back,
           the words that follow each other
           like elephants along a path that
           only they can see, and they trust it
           with every ounce of a million pounds of life.

We're moving in a machine
that sets whole countries
    a mere day apart, but still,
my hand across your thigh, and it means everything,

that one gesture,
    that ease,
           my fingers spread out like I'm playing an octave with one hand.

You are in control of the car.
The miles roll under us, the road
is Aristotle's dream of road,
every mile the same as the last.

I am writing you who feels me touching your leg,
   and only you
      can see me in the corner of your eye, a crescent moon where I
         have every face I have ever had at once.

Found Poem

On a line from Margaret Laurence's *The Diviners*

At my feet, at a bus stop, a bumblebee and a honeybee
are stinging each other to death. At first I think it's two bees mating,
something I had seen only once: not every bee
has a queen surrounded by a hundred thousand female eunuchs
in the monarchy of a hive; the Bombini, bumblebees,
never gave up motherhood to that degree, and plenty of them pair up
to breed like you and I have done in a selfishness so great
it created more of our own.

Once, in the hot first days of autumn,
out on the soccer pitch, I heard two Bombi fucking in the grass,
buzzing as they did it, and I was afraid for them,
being out on the field where we had come to trample and kick.
So I tried to pick them up as one rich flooding coil
singing the mellifluous bumbling aria of nature and sex.

But they broke away from each other, and one flew off,
while the other let me take it out of bounds and play –

                              and that was it –

                    a coitus interrupted, yes,
but a gene code preserved that would otherwise be lost beneath a pair of cleats.

And isn't it odd that it is not odd to talk of living things this way? These days,
            every object is a kind of page,

                    every life a kind of writing.
I feel comforted, thinking of the unfathomable mystery at the heart of the bee
as piece of paper in a bottle, and on that paper, nothing more than one
                    among an infinite arrangement
                    of words.

The bee is a sentence, a line from a song.

But I know my kind.

Someone arriving after me to wait for the bus
would step on these two insects at war. So I pick them up,
and put them on the lawn away from human feet
so they can settle it in the grass undisturbed.

And I recall the fossil I saw as a child of
two dinosaurs that died together, struggling in the mud,
the carnivore with its arm down the other's throat all the way to its stomach,
the plant eater with its teeth sunk in the predator's shoulder all the way to
the bone,

a poem composed in flesh,
　　　　preserved in stone
　　　　　　　that waited 200 million years for its readers.

When: A Love Poem

When
    at last
a man finds himself
in a poem
where he is both longing
    and longed for,

he sees his balding head;
it doesn't glisten
the way it does
in the security video
    that shoots him in the back
with incriminating light,

nor does it laugh
along with his children
for whom time is not yet
something that eats them up;

neither is it cute
and endearing
and curled in its nest
at the zoo –
    all these things

his balding scalp has been,
but never has he heard that skin
spoken of the way you might
of the wood on an antique desk
where a hand,

resting between letters,
moved in the small circles
the hand moves in as it thinks.

My balding head,
sometimes shaky fingers,
incrementally less durable cock,
the torn muscle in my gut
        that's taking months to heal –

once I would have said forgive me
these, or love me through them
as if they needed what
we mean to each other
to become something someone could love.

Not now.

Let us say the poem is not
what we feel
but what we have learned.

I give you the skin of my belly
where it is soft,
the weakness of my arms,
the fold below my chin,
the never-smooth-again
lines around my eyes,
I, who have taken
all this time.

Jack Kirby

As a kid, I used to stare and stare at the way Jack Kirby drew hands,
those nightmare fingers so compelling, it wouldn't be enough alone to look:
I'd contort my own, and hold them up just to see if I could make them
twist the same.
           If I imagined my hands as a drowning man's hands
clawing at the gunnels of a boat, or the hands of a man of gigantic rage
squeezing a child by the arms, I could.

This was my first lesson in the appreciation of art.

I was so young, nothing had died, so I had yet to understand
the TV news, or Goya's huge-lipped fantasies, or let into my mind
the colossus in Jeffers' poems who split human beings down the middle
with his thumb. Now Jeffers – supervillain of American poetry –
                    he was brilliant – and he hated all mankind.

But Kirby? No,
            though witness and liberator at the death camp's broken gates,
              his arms around stick figures' shoulders,
                he helped the survivors through.
And though it is said he dreamed them all the time, the dead he rarely drew.

So I say it's in the men of stone that bestride his work
              that Jack pencilled both his grief and faith.

In all his muscular, grasping art, I say, he kneels
      beside a graven face up to its neck in earth.
           And there he whispers his three-word prayer:
              Move! (Please, move)
something his own God never bent to do.

Superman

There came a time
when my father did not know
when his stomach was full,

        and finishing a meal
        was the same to his brain
        as closing his eyes on the table.

What an image this is:

        my commanding father, whose finger once imitated the thump
        of a bullet striking my chest
        so I might be educated in the way
        power makes a hammer from a nail,

raiding the fridge in the middle of the day
like he was a teen, or toddler, and growing all over again the body of his youth –

and ahead of him, again in olive green, the soldier waits
to dress the limbs and untamed temper of his father's labouring days,
the soldier who'll perfect the man's betrayal by his industrial king.

I'm drawing Superman over and over,
trying to get that beautiful linear face just right,

like it is in the comics –

        a few lines that bless with an uncle's wink to a nephew in the know,
        and then go grim to reap what a villain sows with his indulgences.

I want it all back.

Here is a picture of my father
    at twenty-eight at his brother's wedding. Look at that face –
    see the anatomical plane of his cheek, clean
    and without a sign of anything but future
          in the wingspan of his smile.

I am not yet born.

The war is over.

The home planet is dust.

I cannot get it right.

They say what needs to be done is clear out the fridge
    so Dad can't overeat, feeding a need that nothing will.

What an image it is –
  my dad opening and reopening the Arctic door of his insatiable want:
  it befits an agony from myth.

I cannot explain it to him; his body
has wrested the mind's knowledge of the body
from the mind – and it has taken even his power to understand that.

He rages at an empty box –
    an unfillable thought consuming him.

This is my father in his solitude.

This is my Superman.

Apostrophe

Hello, Paper People. It is I, your creator,
and we have things to talk about.

When I read poems like this one where
someone is talking with someone else who's only there
because all speech has two sides, I test those poems
with this question:

> is the writer telling the someone they're talking to
> something that that someone already knows?

And if the answer is yes, I say,
then it's not a real imaginary conversation,
and yes, that's faking it.

On the other hand,

it's faking it in the glorious tradition of comic book fakery,
the kind where the teeth-clenching hero is trying to open the jaws
of the trap or the monster and they're saying Must ... break ... **free!**
with sweat all over their faces as if anyone ever wasted
an ounce of precious oxygen to talk to themselves at such a time.

But you all know that; that's why you're here,
> Paper Thor,
>> Paper Iron Man,
>>> Captain Paper America,
>> Superpaperman,
> Cut-out Catwoman,
>> Inked Black Widow,
>>> Two-dimensional Goliath.

We go back a long way,
because it's not just you,
the ones I'm speaking to now,
arranged around my desk,

but earlier drawings of you – cut out
                              and play-acted in adventure after childish adventure
with my younger brother as our only witness.

Then picked up again twenty years later – more – each drawing
a version of you to draw me closer to
whatever it is that exists behind every appearance you ever made.

And now?

Now, I am not a comic book artist
                              and never will be.
Still, I write about you,
still read, still think, still draw, still open and close
                              the scissors around your outlined selves.

It must be like this for pagan gods,
each of them filling every statue,
          every painting, every pile of rocks
                    and private shrine
with the full measure of their glory in a child's birth,
          or the gorgeous terribleness of the wave that swamps a fishing boat,
giving nothing back from the water.

Archive

I only wrote one poem drunk.

It was short.

It went,

> I am
> as the wreck of a ship
> to the adventures of men.
>
> In my abandonment
> I am all I have known.
>
> The beaches of the world
> are littered with legends.
>
> Do not forget me.
> I remain the ribs of love,
> the thought, once again,
> of the sea.

It sounded like the poems my father recited
from his chair in the living room, and it worked
particularly well at readings with people from England,
> or people still in love with the England
> my father was from.

Once, a man punched the air at the end of the poem
the way they punch the air in bars when
the home team puts the game away –
> and he whispered also the small Heyesss!
> of enthusiasm in restraint.

He had a British accent.

I was encouraged.

But the poem left the rotation after a few months
because it started to sound not like itself
but like it was remembering the more vital poem it used to be.

In the spaces within it, I started to hear things like
The sea is only a thought, and,
You know, you've never sailed.

Sometimes I wonder what would have happened
if I got even more drunk that night.

I once heard a poet so loaded on stage that
his numbing lips reduced every syllable
to the gurgle of a school kid at a drinking fountain talking through the water.

Every glorious poem of his printed past became
a splashy gurglemumblehum of pleasure or sorrow
                              that no one understood –

and then, rising out of the flood came a single phrase spoken clear:

                    a boy's desire to be good.

I've remembered him for over thirty years;
                        everyone else that day has long since gone.

I ask myself, What would you want left of yours
if you were the one who was drowning up there?

My drunk poem answers:
                    I am. I am. Do not forget me.

Small as God

How few are the intimacies we need to make up for the missing?

The telephone answers us:

        a voice alone, like a poem.

Hello, reader. Hello.

We cannot reverse my father's brain forgetting his memory –

                cell by cell,

taking its time,

        the way a river erases its water with silt.

You'd hardly notice day by day. He's on the line.
And, full of donated blood and drugs,
he still has it in him to make a list with me of all the things
that had already tried to take his life:

The Imperial Japanese Army, it began,
        a big joke now between son and surviving man.

Acute appendicitis in Singapore.
Cigarettes. Skin cancer. A stroke.
Two heart attacks, the last one only months ago.
The Malayan Peoples' Anti-British Army
                once World War II was done.

More:

        The time that fuel line dropped to the tar, spitting sideways
                sparks and gasoline down Highway 401,
        the drivers behind us trying to let us know
            in the language of signs and mirrors.

We were enjoying ourselves, so I did not mention his ruptured ulcer,
                    when I was ten,
                              and he was never again immortal.

But he had one more:
                              Fifty years of marriage, he said,
                    barely squeezing his words through his wheezy laugh –
                              famous in my childhood as the tooth-clenched laugh
                                                            of a cartoon dog.
Today he whispers,

Catastrophic

          from his hospital bed.

He, who'd placed his fingers across the shores of the world,
he, who willed the final bars of the song of his life to fall
without a last, heroic measure should all that given blood collapse
and pool in the great basin of his veins,

he's saying catastrophic though nothing has exploded
beyond the orbit of the sharpest human sight, but shrunk overnight
to fit what the ordinary eye can hold – and less.

You never know how solitary a single room can be
until it frames the portrait of your reach and grasp.

He clasps the phone (again the phone) and his voice quickens to my ear.
Catastrophic, he says,
          alone, like the first man, who prayed
for the invisible to listen, and,
          having listened,
reply with a word as small as God.

Just So Story

We drove the whole family
through the mountains
in a compact car
just so my father
could pet a dog;

he reached out from the wheelchair
he was belted into and pet the dog
we brought into the blessing and curse
of the last home he knew.

They sedated him well,
and his voice was the voice of a tiny being
wandering the catacombs of his body.
In its smallness, it sounded the way I imagine
the voice of hope aching within the chest
after Pandora slammed down the lid.

He didn't give up, my dad,
and he joked that the drool on his lips
made him most like the dog among us all.

And this is the story of his escape:

He had lost his short-term memory,
but he was still his wily self.
From across the corridor,
he watched the visitors
and the staff key in the code
to open the door until he got it.

But by the time no one was around,
and he had wheeled himself over to the keypad,
he'd forgot.

He could still walk a bit back then,
so finally he just bulled his way out.
He got out of the chair
and he pushed past someone's guest
while the door was open,

                         and he was free.

It took them twenty minutes
to guess he'd made it outside,
and he was caught in the street by a nurse
who chased him down the sidewalk
pushing a wheelchair and calling as she pushed,
Ralph! Come back!
                    Come back!

Today, with his family around him,
Ralph's fingers curl
through the pleasing fur of my dog's neck
like a magician passing a coin across his knuckles.
One of the staff at the Home stops with a camera;
the snapshots will be waiting
when we get back to our place.

This is him with the dog in his lap.
We drove three days over the mountains for this.

Propaganda

What a silence contained the sky
    the morning after 9/11.

as if the atmosphere, oxygen-numb,
        had fled the century in cloudy recollection of itself
                a hundred years away from us. And here.

And then the planes returned
      to shear the air with engines.

I have learned what my father learned
when the Germans sent the Hindenburg on its bad-will tour of Britain
before the war, and a lad playing cricket behind a Yorkshire church
gazed up when the Hindenburg gunned its motors,
    cut them
        and floated overhead, a shadow, swastika-finned, casting a shadow

big as neighbourhoods down from the English blue.
    They were just showing off then – everyone knew –
        showing off what they could do at a sieging height in the heavens

from where no human hand had dared before to kill.

Just Who Do You Fuckers Think You Are?

Saddam Hussein's execution video ends
with Saddam's face a pale stone in the moonlight.

Roll it back, those eyes regain their powers
        and glare at his tormentors,
                including the cell phone and every gaze behind it.

I'd like to think otherwise,
      but my guess is I'd be exactly where I am cast in the smuggled feed,
anonymous among the clamour
        in the presence of a man who'll be remembered
        by how many unremembered, better, ones he killed
        and with so much help in the killing that no one
        writes the history of the place without his name.

Perhaps this is why I have watched the video so many times,
           to probe this disappointing portrait of myself.

Maybe this is why George W. Bush, President of the United States
      who started the war with this video as its monument,
never screened these images
      though the most intimate with conquest he ever got is – look there:

                beneath the condemned man's feet,
                centre stage, a square of wood.

This is the way all villains leave their enemies to their fate –
    and still cannot resist the insult of matters more pressing
                as their excuse not to see it through.

And this is the moment of escape, of course,
    but Saddam has run out of things to get away with.

He thought, in fact, it would be worse:
        when asked how he would leave Iraq when his reign was done,
          he answered once, In pieces.

But he died whole, and on camera:
    the video on my desktop makes of him a statue of computer glass and light.

And after all his shattered visages are dragged to the sand,
and the murals painted over where he frowned like a visionary,
this one remains, the dragon whose last sight declared,

Just who do you fuckers think you are?

a mask at the end of a noose,
    eyes closed,
        gazing upward beneath the lids like one dreaming.

Colour Code

Thirteen years old,
>already past her mother's height, my daughter
opened a new box of candy of the kind she'd always known, and she cried
>>because the brown ones couldn't be found.

She had looked for sweets
>the colours of childhood comfort
>>and instead received bad-bread green and disinfectant yellow,
>>and a kind of teal that almost glowed
>>>like a seabird in an oil spill.

At the corner store the future arrives late,
And the present, stale-dated, is still for sale.

She bought the last box of the old-school kind
>as if she'd saved an antiquity from disaster.

And on that box, these words appear:

>Brown:
>Brown reminds me of chocolate and tree houses.
>The world needs more brown.

So much for that.

This year in our garden, the birds are fewer,
>>the butterfly is a rare thing.
There's less ice on the planet;
>>there's less to trust.

My daughter is thirteen,

    the year the grown-ups in cultures much older than my own

gather for their children,

        and the weight that's only carried when it's gone.

Ghost Wood

This is what I read:
    billions of termites,
    descended from those
    that escaped from the wooden walls
    of packing crates
    in which the US army
    shipped home tanks and field artillery
    through the port of New Orleans
    in World War II and after,
    had hollowed out almost all the city
    before half the city was swept away by flood.

Ghost wood I hear they called it,
    because New Orleans understood
    the way haunting worked,
    wood excavated down to almost nothing
    behind its paint,
    the work of uncountable,
    endlessly moving jaws
    just doing what they had to
    to get by.

You couldn't tell by eye,
    but if you tried, in certain homes,
    you could push your finger
    through a six-inch beam.
    So no one did on purpose.
    Everyone held back,
    hoping it was not so.

A beautiful city,
perhaps America's most beautiful city,
with everyone who lived there afraid
to touch it
in case they brought their houses down
with the barest pressure of their own hands.
That is ghost wood.

And I offer it to you as an image
for any purpose that suits;

for example, consider this poem with the title,
"The Sound of Your Voice in My Life,"

or the first title I gave it years ago:
"It All Began So Well,"

or this one, now my favourite:
"I Remember Us as Happy."

Cell Phone

Don't ring.
Switchblade
of language,
don't open,
don't chime,
don't ring.

Long ago, I broke my vow
to use you for
the momentous call alone:
my wife in labour,
come home,
        come home,
or later our first child
in the hospital.

Long ago, I ordered pizza,
or forgot our needs
in the grocery aisle,
and took your space-age
digits quite in vain.
Don't ring.

In your silence is
my father lodged
among the demented
a mountain chain away,
and word of his dying,
and the promise that I made.
Don't ring.

For you,
the perfect measure,
always know the distance
bad news needs
to leap from mouth to ear
in hiding miles away.
I can barely think
when I think of what you bring.
Don't ring today.
Don't ring.

Spoken Word

Look,

      here's a mini tape

            I found the other day at the back of a desk drawer.

It says "Dad: Yorkshire" on the front.

This is how it sounds:

      Eer oll, see oll, say nought,

      eet oll, drink oll, pay nought,

      buhd if evah thee dooh aught foah nought,

      allaas dooh it foh thee sen.

For the full effect, read that out loud in your best British voice.

It won't be any clearer,

      but feel the pleasure of making your tongue thick

            with the accent the way you hear it.

This is the English that the written word erases,

as it was meant to erase everything dialect

that stands in the way of the legal language of government

that works in paper and whispers

            to turn a nation into a state.

I can hear him now, my dad:

Eeerooll for Hear all,

An if eveah thee dooh aught foah nought –

            and if ever you do anything for nothing –

allaas dooh it foh thee sen –

            always do it for yourself.

I no longer own the technology to play the tape,
                              and even if I did, it's no doubt decayed on the spool,
the way all those tapes have decayed,
         betraying every voice we caught mid-air with a magnet
                              and promised we'd keep alive forever.

I'm not sure he ever believed in what he told me was
                    the Unofficial Motto of the Yorkshireman,
         particularly the part about doing things only for yourself.

Dad did a lot of things for other people,
         and not just going off to war the way he did.
Much more,
         and yet,
when I think of him saying something he really meant, it was,
                    You can only teach people to be ungrateful.

Confessional Poem

Yesterday I wrote a confessional poem,
>   but my wife, who always reads me first, said it was just a journal entry.

It's been years since I was that far from a poem and thought I was that close,
>>>   but I trust her.

Today, before class, a student was zipping through a Rubik's Cube,
>   knuckling the box into panels of many colours, then a couplet,
>>   then one   then many again.

Within two minutes, without looking, he was done.
>   I asked him to do it over so we could all watch, and, having watched,
>>   have something with which to begin the writing of the day.

I wrote that the planes of the cube going in and out of order
>   as the student twisted the game were like the drafts of a poem,

sometimes deliberately torquing towards the opposite of the desired end
>   because the poem is a way we give in to a logic that lives within us
>>   but is not our own.

I was thinking of that poem I couldn't write,
>   an apology I wish I'd made years ago,
>>   and carry with me even though two things are true:

>   the person I would have apologized to is dead now,
>>   and what I want to apologize for is speaking badly of them
>>>   though it was only to my wife and so they never knew.

The poem was like having an argument with someone in a dream,
>   then going up to them in daylight wanting to make amends.

Last time I did that,
    the other person reminded me
        that I had done nothing.

But I apologized anyway
    because they had done nothing
        to deserve what I did not do.

Greatness

My father reciting "Fern Hill" at the midpoint in his life,
his favourite of the Dylan Thomas poems that have him by heart,

fades in the aging machine I can play it in. Listening to it
is like watching a vase fall to the floor in slow motion.

Listening to it is to learn the immortality that was promised
by machines that hold our images and speech till we want them again

is nothing more than the fashion of the day for its technology of record –
a mirror posing for itself and laughing at the way things used to be.

This is how I remember it. My father's voice is lyric and soft,
schooled by Dylan but lacking Dylan's church bell grief.

The poet read from his feet as he steadied himself with words whose weight
he could hardly bear. But Dad read from the column of his torso and the plinth

of his hip bones as though a child was sleeping next to him whose dreams
he whispered into but would not dream of waking.

I have heard him recite the poem for years, but when he reached "Fern Hill's"
conclusion while I recorded, and he spoke that *Time held me green and dying*

Though I sang in my chains like the sea, his eyes broke and his mouth knew
no shape but a moan. A line can sum a life. And this was his.

Soon we would all leave the house and the family. A line like that cracks open
what a man puts all his faith in so he can do the work. And maybe that is art.

Or vanity. Or pride. Or sacrifice, or secrets, or the belief his children will
someday be better than himself. Such a line as contains the life and still has
room left over,

that line sweeps everything into nothing and still declares, Well? a greatness
my father could not answer.

With the Dying of the Light

I recited to him,

        Now as I was young and easy,

and in the cough-afflicted wheeze that was left of my father's voice,

              he answered, under the apple boughs,

and so it went between us

    in the days I waited for him to recover –

        the way hope pillows its sails with nothing –

            or falter, fade and pass away.

You haven't heard

    Time held me green and dying

    Though I sang in my chains like the sea

        until you've heard it from the wizened mouth

        of a man in the not-knowing-when before his death.

This is the reply to the poet

    who longs for the old man to rage at the night,

        and heed his child's plea, Don't go!

My father's was the soft song of sickened lungs,

    lips that lost the taste for even one more swallow

        while I waited with him in the light that faded as it drew close.

I saw him from the doorway, silent as a mummy,

    his hands locked into each other like power shovels

        tipped into the posture of the day's last work,

  the crew gone home for the night.

Once, he waved after days of Shakespeare and Dickens,
      the anthem of literature he had been taught to love
            as his country itself,

and through which he spoke best
      the savage and gentle contradictions of his heart.

I'd said, I love you,
      and he'd said, I love you, too,
            without the artifice of poetry;

and he waved when I moved from the bed
      the way a boat, pushed by a hand gone still on the dock,
                carries yet its force across the water.

It is here now, what that hand held when it held itself up,
            the lull before the poem begins,
                the surrender when it's done.

Ode to a Temporary Urn

After my father was burned,
    I stood with his ashes in the room where he once slept,
        the ashes in two plastic jars divided – one for my brother, one for me,

each the same jar you get when you buy energy drink as a powder,
            or the minerals the body needs but we often fail to give it.
Shaken,

it rattles like pebbles and sand.
    They tell you no one is ready for how heavy the remains are
        that measure God's hand at His work in the dust.

They're right. The container proclaims,
      Not for Permanent Use,
        and though it is efficient,
      this temporary urn is not a thing of beauty,
        so it tells me nothing joyful about forever:

Immortality is nothingness,
    an absence absolute, and so great
      it becomes presence and its opposite at once.

The jar is perfect.

All my life I have loved my father,
    and I have this now, a love I never knew until he was gone, and I held him.

The Creative Writing Teacher Writes to His Wife

One of my students is living with cystic fibrosis,
>   and he loves the poem.

Today he found himself at the limit
>   of what the poetry he's written so far can hide,
>   and if he wants to write more, it has to be of this.

He's telling me for the first time,
>   and this is not about pity,
>   though pity is the first fall I take.

We were talking.
I saw my son
with the same tight mouth,
and the young man and my son and I
all born helpless in order to become men
the way birds are born naked
so they can fly.

I said to him, Speak of your life.
>   Teach everyone who thinks they've got the whole long world ahead.

I was thinking of our son,
>   shouting to his friends across an electric landscape
>   from the rooftop of his voice,

and my father, dying with his mouth open
>   and the rhythmic pondering sound the dying make
>   until the drugs settled him down to die quiet.

Borges: "The Riddle of Poetry"

Borges said the truest reading of the poem is the first.
When this poem proves him right, I will stop revising.

I wanted a poem. I found no words.
Borges said, *every time I am faced with a blank page,*
I feel that I have to rediscover literature. OK, then. I want more.
I will begin with Borges, and rediscover his voice for a start.

The poem cannot be an expression,
Borges said, for if it were, you could ask,
Of what? the same question you could ask of life.
Neither has an answer other than itself.

Once at a writers' retreat, the poet on the other side of our shared wall
cast me as Borges in a poem – and Borges was twins:
one that everyone saw, the other who never left the room.
But the poet heard them talking,
           so the poet knew the truth.

And now, Borges is reading this poem out loud.

A Home on Al-Mutanabbi Street

I am a word. I am a word in Arabic, in English and in Farsi. I am a word in
Kurdish and German and Hebrew and French. I am a word in the mouths
of prophets and hawkers. I will get you tea. I will bring you joy and to tears.
I am a word in a book. I lie open to the sun that reads me over the shoulder
of someone looking to buy. I am the imagination of the enemy come home
to its enemy's understanding because the leap from enemy to friend is as
swift and sure as the journey from paper to eye. I am loved. I am reviled.
I am feared. I am myself and I am you. When the book opens, you can hear
me sigh in pleasure at the touch of your mind. When the bombs go off,
      I am scattered
                from all that I have known,
                                and the wind and ashes take me.

          You might think I disappear, but I do not.

      The fires die down,
              my place in the house,
                    on the street, in the rebuilt café remains.

                        I am memory and the stuff of memory.
                I survive the past because I am always the present.
      I survive death because I am the future.
I survive hatred because I am love.

      Build me a home,
              and I will return and be heard.
And when you see me filling the page again,
             you will know I never abandoned you.

More Sex, More Nature

A poem for Lisa on our Nineteenth Anniversary

Today on our balcony,
> we were talking about my poems.

>> More sex, more nature, you say.

Let me in.

In the garden below us,
> the sunflower stalks stiffen their seedy heads.
> I am greedy for the mouths of poetry and words spoken
> in ways they have never been spoken before.
I want to learn the body anew the way a great fuck
> teaches me new things about the flesh I dumbly thought I knew.
> Sometimes I rise from our bed and wonder if it was really me.

Everything is nature and sex,
> everything is continuance.

I would have told you the opposite
> before you, before children.

> A self is a tiny thing, filled so full on so few words,
> and made hungry by so much
> for more.

The Golden Age

The man who wrote my favourite childhood comics
                         said, The Golden Age for everything is 8.

        My son is ten, the dusk of his belle époque

The light from every slow-falling sun makes even the tiniest leaf,
                         angled just right, glint the story of its descent.

In such a spangle in the corner of my eye, my
        boy didn't like Captain America: The First Avenger as much the second time,
though we saw it twice that week in the theatre,
                         that's how thrilled we'd been.

Take the scene where the freshly minted supersoldier
                         lives the dream of every grade-school kid
and catapults himself over the prison fence that surrounds the yard
                 without even touching the top –
                         a leap to test our faith and leave nothing in its wake but awe.

And it did – once.

Seeing it again, my son said it was just a man
                         pretending to be a cartoon.

I always look for hope. In my most fatherly voice, I say,
        Congratulations. You're harder to please. You're getting a critical eye.

But he is inconsolable: I hate that eye, he says,
        And this where hope can take you: I leap to the defence
of the critical pleasure of the poem dissected in class
        whose body even its author couldn't claim in the morgue of the analyzed.

My voice is almost priestly,

       the way every voice is clear and precise

       when the speaker wants God in his heaven

       and all to be right in the world but knows that none of that is true –

              even in the smallest thing.

My son has found a new discontent, and it is too soon.

Still, I hope again, and say,

     You see more than you used to see.

     Now you have more to be happy about

     when things are truly good.

But he has the comeback for that as well:

     *I liked it better when **everything** was good,*

And then there we are together

     with nowhere to go but farther away,

         side by side

            within sight of the paradise

               on the other side of criticism.

Epic

The body he thought about every day
was the one its own blood could not warm.

He felt as if he was always late,
or there was somewhere else he should be.

Give me more, he wished.
                    Give me something else.
Let me see him with his hair black as boots,
at ease with the bigness of his hands.

Let me see him through
            the epic failures in his love
the way he did who wrote of him
            in the beautiful blindness of the poem.

Saddledome: After the Flood

This is the Ark after the Flood:
> hull full of water, the animals gone.

I feel more for Noah after this,
> getting drunk every night since dry land
>> knowing dry land as a faith that would never return.

Water is complicated:
> see how brown in these pictures it is,
>> how full of the earth it leaves behind when the river packs up
>>> and heads back to bed.

That's microbial brown,
> fertility,
>> earthworm realm,
> the colour of the soil that binds with naked feet.
.

**

I love the parabola in its roof,
> the Saddledome: I'll miss it when they build
>> the next entertainment colossus

and the game is something someone is doing in one room
> while the television is on in another.

Remember the days
when everyone gathered around the set to eat
> because anything on was only on then?

The Saddledome remembers, and those days were not so long ago,
             though they became far, far away in a flash
      like the time you dropped your car keys down the sewer.

After the flood, I saw a lovely 42-inch television
      sitting on a dolly outside someone's home, and I thought,
             even if that TV was brand new, what I want to steal is the dolly.

**

After the flood,
      my basement was the Event Level of the Saddledome,
             water up to the expensive seats, shelves full of the books I read
      while I was finding my writing voice, boxes of archives
                    in torrential disarray.

I feel for the Dome.

I feel for Theo Fleury
      hurling himself like a takeout-weight curling stone the length of the ice,
             arms pumping in a hockey joy so great
                    he forgot for a moment his suicidally crippling secrets –

What I want is that joy in the poem.
      The best lines from thirty years of paper tossed afloat
             are the ones I dismissed or misread when I saw them.

Consider: Sometime in the early 1980s I handwrote,

Is this art
that I have mastered it so quickly?

When I took it from the blur of water,
I read it out loud and said instead,

Is this art, that I have misunderstood it so soon?
and it became a line for a poem at last.

Poetry is play, even in the darkest of its discontents.
Poetry is a sex abuse victim,
        shoulders back, roaring out the body alive,
and rhyme is the laughter of disasters we survive.

That's why the hockey book was the door for me
from saying to writing,
        from myself to the poem,
from me to you.

That's why.

Under Western Water: Returning to Work

My books stood by the water resting at their wooden shore,
   and they were patient and quiet and the water had stopped
     rising in my house and in the houses of all my neighbours.

The books reminded me of penguins waiting at the icy edge of the sea,
   none of them wants to be first in case there's a leopard seal
       under the surface.
Sooner or later (we've all seen the films), one of them falls –
   if it lives, the rest go in because it's safe,
     if it dies, the rest go in because the seal isn't hungry anymore.

Sometimes when I'm walking across a bridge,
   I feel that strange gravity that says, Go on, you want to,
  and when I think of all those books with their spines and their silence,
I feel the anger of parents who shout at children
     who don't get hit by cars even though they walked
     into the street without looking.

I say, The water was right there
   and my books looked like they were standing on the shore,
    and my friends, whose love you can measure in their listening,
   smile and say, You're writing a poem, aren't you?

More words is the answer to the fact that a book,
fallen into the water,
takes the same second between life and death
to be ruined by its own pages.

A piece of paper born to soak up all the meaning
that ink can give will take a drink from any water it's offered,
and then it will bloat, and relieve itself of everything it held.

Where I didn't save them,
> the books thickened so much with water
>> they split their shelves.

**

I moved around the flooded basement.
> Things drifted between the bookshelves
>> and the submerged futon and the darkened warping boards
>>> of the piano that was slowly being destroyed.

Some of those things were cards we'd saved from all card-occasions:
birthday cards and anniversary cards, and congratulations and sickness
and every one of those cards was blank
because the card stock shed all its ink into the water
> and all the meaning was let go.

So I read them as sympathy cards from the river, saying,
Sorry. I couldn't have done anything else. I'm sorry.

And I was not moving in the basement,
just standing, waiting for the ripples I had made to go still.

It's like that moment when the therapist asked,
> How did you feel? and I answered,
>> I was thinking about being small, about being nothing,

and there I found the blank place in my mind
> that has winked open every so often ever since,
>> even in the middle of the working day.

I'll be typing a letter,
　　　　and I'll look away from the screen
　　　　　　　and look back and wonder what I was typing,
and who was waiting for me,
　　　　　　　　　　but that's not where I was going.

**

I was going to tell you
　　　　that sometimes the water itself just moved –
　　　　　　　　　　it rose a little at one end of the room,
　　　　　　　like something tilted the house from below.
　　　And there it was, the proof: I was standing in a tiny part
of a mass of water that connected
　　　　　　all the cities and towns and villages along the river,
　　　　　　　　water that spread over the city,
　　　remaking it,
　　　drawing a new topographical waterline all over it
　　　　　　with everything below that line wounded.

I was in the body of a great silent beast,
　　　　the landscape, and the waterway,
　　　　　　　and the rain revealing itself at once
　　　　　　　　　from behind civilization's enormous forgetting.

Maps and Writing Paper

Imagine the unfenced land of Southern Alberta
                        without chart or prediction.
                                It's still somewhere
                                        you can go.

Everything has already been written
            yet I still write as if there is something new to find.

I need words close, as though I matter to them,
                        even though I don't.

The new blank page says,

> Here, write here; I am nothing without the work of your pen,
> empty but for the conjuring gesture of your fingers.
> I am the hole,   the gap,   the crack.   I am vacant land.
> Move in, set up house, draw your mind back and forth
> like furrows.
>   Grow a family,
>   the page fills up like the land
>   because the land fills up like the map.

And this is why Nothing is something in our language,
                not just a word for infinite subtraction, but a place
                        for all the work we have to do.

The paper is bridal white,
        terra nullius
                and the map of lands unchristened by makers of maps
    the colour of
            no one's home,
                    the colour of, Take me, I'm yours.

Skype

Last night I dreamed I was Skyping with my father.
I could see him up close, and he was far away.

>We talked about how far away I was.
>Our devices rewrite us. I see my dreams like Skype.

Once I would have said it was like I was an angel or he was a ghost.
Once I would have said

>he was on a TV that let me talk
>>with the person on the screen.

>But then "Impossible TV" would be all I'd have
>to express that strange clarity at distances
>>once the scripture of dreams and revelations.
>>Now it's the software.

I am waiting for the next near-death experience to be explained in that
language –

>I was on the operating table, the returned soul says,
>the light at their back, and it was like I was Skyping with my own body.

My father will never say he is sad,
>but I can tell that he has not yet finished mourning my loss.

Instead he says,
>It's been a long time since we talked.

This Poem is Alive Because it is Unfinished

My father is alive, I dared to type, and there he was:
                            my father, who blew kisses to the young women
            who tended him in his infirmary bed,
            and fed him what he could drink of the world in its last paper cups.

My father loved as a mouth loves.
            He called them my darlings, and they giggled,
                being shy and familiar with sorrow, and they told me, He's our favourite,
                            when they left us alone together.

The hours of my father's dying taught me
                the older you get, the more emotions you feel, each harder to
                describe, and the differences between them.

They said, He's our favourite,
                            and by those words I recall them.

Maybe he was, maybe he wasn't;
            maybe they say that to everyone who visits the dying
                        in their care – it does not matter.

When I believe them, it is the same as when I don't,
            their words no longer burdened with the ordinary business
                of telling me something I should know.

Even the most powerful among us fall asleep,
                            or become ill, or just stop whatever it is they're doing
                                            and stand a while.

Sometimes a poem can let us see our love in a new light,
                the way my dying father does when he can do no more.

This poem is alive because it is unfinished.
My father is alive,
      and I am holding his hand,
          and his hand is pale, and blue, and violet,
               a trembling garden of irises.

A Poem is a Story that Sometimes Happens to Someone

I dreamt I slept with a former lover,
and woke up not knowing if I had dreamed about what I had done
before I knew you, or remembered in my sleep
a time she and I went and fucked like we were young again
and had nowhere else to go.

There are no clocks in dreams;
we all live together on the planet of memory.
Who knows who will meet whom? or when?
the living and the dead,
them preserved in anger turned to stone,
the unloved and the loved.

I wake up and there you are,
sleeping with your mouth open
the way the open mouth is pretty
on someone caught thinking
the nothing they are thinking
between their thoughts.

I want to wake you up and ask you to forgive me –
first, for what I did in the dream, then for enjoying it so much.
Then for my doubt.

I've never mentioned dreams like this,
or how the first one of its kind troubled me for weeks.

I've never let myself write them down where they could be seen,
or (until right now) read aloud.

There are parts of myself I've kept from the light,
and been the lesser for having done so.

On one of those walks
　　　where we become clear with each other,
　　　　　　our son tells me he doesn't **get** poetry,
but he keeps my books against the day when he will be old enough to read them.

He tells me he thinks a poem is a story
　　　　　　that sometimes happens to someone,
　　　　　　　　　and asks me if that is right.
I say he gets my poems,

　　　and he's more right than he knows.

Birthday Card

In 1939, like thousands of English children, my mother
was sent from London for fear Hitler would attack the city.

She was sent to a farm, far away from harm, or so it was supposed to be.
Instead, she was sexually abused by the father of that house.

She was returned home because her parents, like many, found the separation
worse than the fear of falling bombs, and some said London would be spared.
Then came the Blitz.

My mother's mind never let go of her anger at the Germans, but what
her body never forgot or forgave, I think now, on my birthday, was men.

Five years after my father died, she's happier than I've ever seen her.
She's smaller, she uses a walker, but she's light around the shoulders,

and the edges of her mouth – she makes more jokes. And though men are her
doctor and ophthalmologist, and though men take care of her teeth, mend her

broken bones, have repaired or removed her internal organs, though men take
care of her apartment and drive her everywhere, though men are the only children

she's got, and every day reinforces that men are in charge, her body
is much happier now that all of us are in charge at a distance.

I wouldn't have understood any of this until I saw her the other day,
glad to be alive, her tables adorned with assembled and assembling puzzles,

which are pictures of pride in its most innocent form. I have often thought of
my mother's life as a kind of defeat that never got over itself,

but today I am fifty-nine years old, and my body, failing my expectations,
is something I am happy at last to call my own without holding back.

I am looking at my mother. I am learning about time, and how time
would never have begun if she had given up and not let me be born.

Prayer

My father taught me the poem was a bed of gravel
                  the rain could not wash away,
                                a sheet of particleboard cut clean with a knife –
                                not a saw,
                  the sideways glance you use to find a contact lens on the carpet.

Poetry was touching the hiker in front of you
                        in the small of the back so you both make it up the hill.

My father went to war with his head full of English verse,
            but although he spoke with them, the language of
                        King George's soldiers he fought with
side by side,
            he taught me only these words of theirs:
                                  Sat Sri Akaal: God is Truth.

The Wonder of Life

Once, I watched a praying mantis eat a snake.
This was decades ago, and soon I would be leaving the woman
                              I'd promised to live with forever.

The mantis ate the snake like a shredder eating a sausage,
                    and all I saw was the end of things.

But I am in our house today,
        and mantis and snake are loose from the meaning that once held them.

Genus Mantis waited 100 million years for its first reptile lunch.
                                      And liked it.

Over time, flesh folded this way and that,
            everything born with a taste for the future.

Even then, you were on your way, and after that, our children.

The answer is: Be patient.

I saw a praying mantis eat a snake.

              There is hope for us all.

Mulligan

In memoriam for my father-in-law, Phil Rouleau

My virgin shot
        from the first tee at the Royal Regina

                took off straight for the spectators,
                        hit a tree,
            bounced back

      with a crack
    like a nail gun,

and landed thirty feet behind me.

Here's the thing about golf: It's impossible
           to exaggerate how badly you've done.
So it's the sport that's most like life.

It takes a certain kind of mind to play the game.
To love it is something else again.

I wanted to change the world – and get things right.
Phil wanted to love the world as it was – and do his best.

Thirty feet is not a long way – until it's backwards.
           The ball nested in the grass, the egg of shame.
The silence was so full, you could have walked on it –
           and Phil must have because I didn't hear him
           until he stood beside me, a new ball in his hand.

Yoda said, Do or do not. There is no try.
Yoda never played golf.
Yoda was wrong.

For proof, I offer Phil's wisdom that kept me in that game,
         and in how many more I cannot say since then:
                That happens, he said. Try again.

Haiku

I have never been adept at haiku,

but I keep returning to this one.

It would be easy to dismiss my frustration with a joke:

It demands haiku,
bee within chrysanthemum.
Damn. I got nothing.

But that quits the moment
and the moment is too much a moment to quit –

a honeybee dormant in a luxurious flower
on a cold March morning,
the sun barely touching the petals,
my wife and I walking along just then.

And there's the insect
vulnerable and asleep
where it chose to hide itself when the cold came on,
and it knew there was no way back to the hive in time.

And the flower, cradling the bee,
the instrument of its own propagation,
in the shapes and scent it used to bring it there.
The bee in the flower looks exotic,
like a clownfish in an anemone,
but there it is, by the sidewalk,
in a neighbour's garden in the ordinary light.

Is that what haiku is?

a bee noticed in a flower?

Basho said yes,
     and my favourite haiku is still his:

                      A bee
                 staggers out
                of the peony.

Maybe it's in the verb.
     Maybe I'm looking for a word
          that does for sleep what staggers does for walk.

The bee snoozes?
          dozes?
                    dreams?

But if I am,
     then am I not just trying to be Basho? –
            and what's the point of that?

You learn and try, then you unlearn and do.

It isn't about the flower or the bee.
It isn't about haiku,
or the prose poem,
a little story that goes nowhere
except, if you're lucky, to aha!

It's about the one thing you notice,
              and then the why: yes, a bee, thumbed into a flower
         by the cold of a night still unburned away by the morning sun.

A man walking with his wife,

but not walking with her in his mind, instead looking away
and down, taking things in with his eyes.

Perhaps he is thinking;
        perhaps he has just said something, and he's waiting for her
                to say something back.

She is holding his hand,
        but he has let go of the thought of holding hers,
                        and something has got his attention,

something connected to what's happened before he saw it
                        in a way he could not speak of at the time.

And now he's writing,
                        connecting before and after through now.

Experience is to a poem what a belly button is to a mammal.

Bees sleep in flowers all the time.

Dormant in a million darkened books,
                        poems wait for someone to lift their caps.
        The man knows that everything he writes
                will eventually become patient like them
        as if he never wrote what he writes now:

                At last the man sees
                the poem is the woman's hand
                resting in his own.

Acknowledgements

Thank you to Noelle Allen, Ashley Hisson, Emily Dockrill Jones and
Joe Stacey of Wolsak and Wynn for their many years' support of my work.
Thanks to my fellow poets in Calgary's Thursday Group for the weekly tests
of poetry and poetic thinking. Likewise to my students at Mount Royal
University who constantly ask my old knowledge to answer new questions.
And to Beth Everest, Betsy Struthers, David Eso, derek beaulieu, Kelly
Hewson, Larissa Lai, Micheline Maylor, Shelley Youngblut, Sheri-D Wilson
and Weyman Chan, my thanks for the constancy of your friendship and
fellow love of this art.

To Paul Vermeersch, the most hands-on editor it's been my pleasure to work
with. Without you, these poems would never have the breadth or the breath
that they have now, nor would this book have been the change in my work
my father's life and death deserved to effect in it.

To my mother, who first showed me that the book was the place where words
waited to be awakened, and in whose voice live the great characters and
dramas of my childhood's first literature.

To my dad, who, even in his last years when he could no longer articulate
a response to poems, would listen to these on the phone and whisper from
time to time for a line, "uh hmm" or "that's good."

And to my family: my children, Emma and Keeghan Harrison Rouleau,
who've never stopped being as inspiring as they were from the moment they
were born, and who still cut through the literary clutter in my mind straight
to that which is artistic and honest in the words. And Lisa Rouleau, who
knows me best, reads me first and loves me with that love that never settles
for anything but the truth.

Notes

These poems, or earlier versions of them, have appeared in the journals
FreeFall, Canadian Literature, Big Pond Rumours and Eyewear (UK),
as well as the anthologies Al-Mutanabbi Street Starts Here, Where the
Nights are Twice as Long, The Calgary Project: A City Map in Verse and
Visual, and the high school textbook Modern Morsels: Selections of Canadian
Poetry and Short Fiction. "Just So Story" was shortlisted for the inaugural
Montreal International Poetry Prize. An earlier version of "Poem for a
Crescent Moon" won the Alberta Magazine Publishers Association (AMPA)
2013 Award (Silver), and "Confessional Poem" won the AMPA 2016, Gold.

The quotations from Shakespeare (Richard III) and Dylan Thomas
("Fern Hill" and "Do Not Go Gentle into that Good Night") were among
the literature my father and I quoted to each other all my life. The opening
monologue from the play and the lines from the poetry were among the
readings we shared while he was on his deathbed.

My father died November 1, 2011, of vascular dementia, the third most
common form of mental deterioration after Alzheimer's and Lewy Body
Dementia, both of which, at times, Dad was diagnosed with. Even then
the disease wasn't as well known as it is now; in the end, his condition
was settled by the fact that he lived longer than the other two conditions
would have let him, a deciding factor that he would have found, like the
loss of his ashes, worthy of a good laugh.

In terms of property and ecosystemic damage, the Alberta flood of
June 2013 was, at the time, the single largest disaster in Canadian history.
It was the result of an unprecedented confluence of weather-related events.
My neighbourhood was flooded as water from the Bow swept back from
the river through the storm drains and gushed up, like a fountain show,

filling the lowlands like a bowl. If you have the *Maclean's* magazine issue devoted to the flood, and you hold open the two-page photo taken from McHugh Bluff overlooking downtown, your right thumb is on top of my house.

The Robert Hass poem referenced in the title work in this book is "August Notebook: A Death."

All the accounts of the Slinky's origin agree with the National Toy Hall of Fame's version of a tension coil falling from a shelf above Dick James's desk in 1943. But Jay Morehouse's 1948 newspaper story implies that James's office was on board a ship at sea at the time. I like that it may be the ocean itself that caused the discovery of a toy that's essentially a metal wave.

The line from Margaret Laurence's *The Diviners* in "Found Poem" is from "Morag does not reply. She is watching two flies fucking, buzzing while they do it." These sentences were part of the "evidence" mustered by Canada's religious right in the early 1980s that Margaret's work was sexually arousing, and thus not fit for high school English students.

"When: a Love Poem" is, in part, a response to and the result of Jim Nason's poetry about the male body in *Narcissus Unfolding*.

"Small as God" owes a debt to Robert Hilles' poem "God is the Smallest Object" from *Cantos from a Small Room*.

Terra nullius – "no one's land" in "Maps and Writing Paper" refers to the designation of lands not ruled by Christians under the eleventh-century papal doctrine by that name. The poem owes much to Haida manga artist Michael Nicoll Yahgulanaas's political and aesthetic critique of the gutter between panels in comics, said to be the "empty space" the reader's imagination requires to bring the sequence of pictures to life.

The article referred to in "Ghost Wood" is Duncan Murrell's 2005 account "The Swarm" in Harper's magazine. I'm not certain where I heard the term *ghost wood*, but to my surprise, it isn't there, nor, except for a New Orleans punk band, have I been able to go back and link its use to that city. Maybe I made it up, but it feels like something that ought to be true, even if it isn't.

In the Borges poem, the subtitle "The Riddle of Poetry" is Borges's own title for the first lecture in the series he gave at Harvard in 1967 and 1968, which he published as *This Craft of Verse*. The poem mentioned at the end is by Toronto poet Jim Smith.

"A Home on Al-Mutanabbi Street" appears in the anthology *Al-Mutanabbi Street Starts Here*, and on a broadside created by Trisha Eddy, with an Arabic translation by Antoine Sassine. This work, along with the work of hundreds of artists around the world, is part of San Francisco poet Beau Beausoleil's project to continue the struggle against those whose minds are revealed and actions symbolized by the car-bomb destruction of the Baghdad street that was home to a printing press/café and that city's thriving and non-sectarian book-loving community.

The writer quoted at the front of "The Golden Age" is Roy Thomas, who took the reins of writing and editing for Marvel Comics after Stan Lee left. Where Kirby was epic, and Lee a comedian, Thomas was one of the early writers to shape superhero stories around the forms of literary fiction.

It is Robert Hass's translation of Basho's "A Bee" that appears in the poem "Haiku."

Richard Harrison's eight books include the Governor General's Award–finalist Big Breath of a Wish, and Hero of the Play, the first book of poetry launched at the Hockey Hall of Fame. He teaches English and Creative Writing at Calgary's Mount Royal University, a position he took up after being the Distinguished Writer-in-Residence at the University of Calgary in 1995. His work has been published, broadcast and displayed around the world, and his poems have been translated into French, Spanish, Portuguese and Arabic. In On Not Losing My Father's Ashes in the Flood, Richard reflects on his father's death, the Alberta Flood and what poetry offers a life lived around it.